Trainee Handbook

BY **JimWiese** WITH **H.KeithMelton**
SPY EXPERT

SCHOLASTIC INC.

NEW YORK TORONTO LONDON AUCKLAND SYDNEY
MEXICO CITY NEW DELHI HONG KONG BUENOS AIRES

ISBN 0-439-33639-2

Copyright © 2002 by Scholastic Inc.

Editor: Andrea Menotti
Designer: Lee Kaplan   Illustrations: Daniel Aycock
Photos: H.K. Melton

21   6 7 / 0

Printed in the U.S.A.

First Scholastic printing, September 2002

The publisher has made every effort to ensure that the activities in this book are safe when done as instructed.
Children are encouraged to do their spy activities with willing friends and family members and to respect others'
right to privacy. Adults should provide guidance and supervision whenever the activity requires.

TABLE OF Contents

👓 **This means you'll use your Spy Gear in this activity.**

💻 **This means you can find a related activity on the Spy University web site.**

Welcome

Hey, can you keep a secret? Can you uncover one? What about the hidden message on this page—can you find it? Have a look! (You can get a hint on page 48.)

All kinds of great secrets await you here at Spy University. If you want to be *in the know*, then you've come to the right place, and your training begins now!

As a Spy University trainee, you'll learn the skills spies use to find secrets and keep them safe. You'll learn how to watch like a spy, how to listen like a spy, and how to make and break codes like a pro. You'll find out how spies disguise themselves, how they hide their cameras, how they make maps and take notes, how they catch enemy spies, and how they avoid getting caught themselves.

And there's a lot more in store for you, too. You've started a course of study that'll make you a full-fledged, ready-for-anything spy!

ABOUT THIS BOOK

This is your handbook, your first step toward spyhood. Flip through the pages, and you'll find lots of activities (otherwise known as your "missions" or "operations"), along with stories of real-life spies, photos of gadgets, and other great features that'll introduce you to the secrets of the spy world. Then, each month after this, for as long as you're a Spy University trainee, you'll get another book that focuses in detail on one area of spy technique.

Here's what you're getting this month:

YOUR MISSIONS

In this book, you'll find out how to set up and secure your spy headquarters. Then you'll take on a variety of missions (if you choose to accept them!) that will develop your skills in surveillance, communications, disguises, escapes, secret codes, and more. You'll even try your hand at spy catching!

SPY TOOLS AND TALES

You'll get to read the stories of real-life spies and see actual photos of the special gear they use. This month's Spy Feature will take you back in time and around the world in search of the roots of modern-day spying.

to SPY UNIVERSITY!

SPY QUEST

Here's where you'll get a chance to sharpen your spy skills. Your Spy Quest adventure begins with an opening scene (which you'll find on page 11) that introduces a case for you to handle. You'll then have to make a decision about what to do first. After you decide, you'll turn the page, see the consequences of your actions, and decide what to do next. Will you be able to solve the case quickly? Or will you make a mistake, end up at a dead end, and have to start all over again? It's all based on your choices, so try to decide wisely!

SPY GEAR

What's a spy book without the gadgets? Not much, right? So, you've got:

● **A Spy Case** for your gear. It's got plenty of straps and pockets to hold the gadgets you'll be getting in upcoming months (like a mini-camera, a listening device, and lots more).

● **A Spy Guard motion detector** to help keep your headquarters (and your stuff) secure. It's disguised as a key chain, so it's an *undercover* Spy Guard.

● **An ID Badge kit** to make your own Spy University credential.

● **A telescope/microscope device called a Telemicro.** And guess what—it's disguised as a pen! When it's in one piece, you can use it as a telescope (slide out the bottom tube to focus it). To use it as a microscope, separate the two parts and look through the top part or the hollow bottom tube. The bottom part is good for magnifying tiny writing and fingerprints. Use the top part for an even closer (but upside-down) view.

TELESCOPE

Top Part

Bottom Part

MICROSCOPES

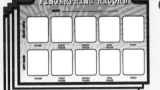

● **A set of four fingerprint cards** for your spy records.

OTHER MUST-HAVES FOR YOUR SPY TRAINING

▼ **A notebook to record your observations.** If you choose one that's small enough, you can keep it inside your spy case.

▼ **A spy network**—that is, some friends and family to join you in your spy training and take part in your missions.

5

SPY UNIVERSITY WEB SITE

But wait, there's even more! Your Spy Gear kit also includes a secret password card that'll give you access to the Spy University web site at **www.scholastic.com/spy**. There you'll find lots of great on-line challenges and games designed exclusively for spies-in-training like you. Be sure to sign in soon—but don't forget your password (which you can also find right here in the Password Spot), because only Spy University trainees have clearance to enter the site.

So, enjoy your handbook! Learn lots, and come back for more, because each month after this, you'll get another book that focuses in depth on one area of spy **tradecraft** (that's what spies call the set of techniques they use). Here are some tradecraft areas that you'll be getting to know:

- Secret codes and ciphers
- Spy security
- Surveillance
- Counterintelligence
- Undercover communications
- Escape and evasion
- Hiding places
- Scouting and reconnaissance
- Disguises, covers, and legends
- Uncovering secrets

Some of these words might sound strange to you at first, but stick with us, and soon enough you'll know how to talk the talk and walk the walk! Now move on to the next page and start your training with a quick introduction to the basics of the spy world.

P.S. A word to wise spies Sometimes (we'll tell you when), you'll need to have an adult (also known as a "senior spy") with you when you perform your spy missions. Don't forget that! It's an important Spy University rule. Also, do these activities with your friends and family, in safe places. *Good* **spies are always** *wise* **spies!**

spybasics

H ere's a little introduction to the **who**, **what**, **where**, **when**, **how**, and **why** of the spy world, otherwise known as the world of **espionage**.

Who are Spies?

Spies are men and women of all descriptions. To begin with, they need to be very smart and well-educated (so keep doing that homework, spy trainee!), and then they learn a very specific set of skills for spying—like the ones you'll be learning at Spy University. Spies are not necessarily glamorous or rich, or dressed in the finest clothes (or sneaky-looking trench coats, hats, and sunglasses) like spies in the movies. In fact, a good spy will blend into the crowd and attract as *little* attention as possible!

What Do Spies Do?

The basic job of a spy is to collect information. Unlike what you might see in the movies, spies don't actually go around killing people. Real spies have to do the opposite—that is, they have to connect with people, forge friendships, and build trust, so they can get someone who knows a secret to share it. Even the best spies would have a tough time getting information out of a dead person!

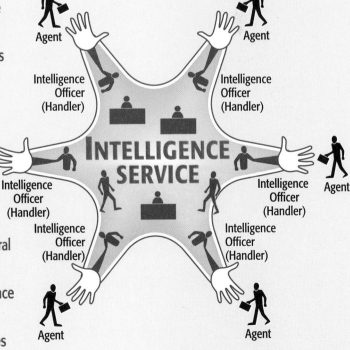

Where Do Spies Work?

Spies usually work as **agents** for a government's **intelligence service** like the Central Intelligence Agency, or CIA, in the United States. Agents aren't official employees of the intelligence service. (That's why they're sometimes called *secret* agents—get it?) They're chosen to be spies by **intelligence officers** (who *are* employees of the intelligence service) because they have access to secret information.

Agents usually live and work in one country, secretly gathering information on behalf of another country. The information they collect is used to help the government they work for make decisions about how to handle relations with other countries, how to fight (and avoid) wars, how to prevent terrorism, and so on.

Spying isn't always international, though. Spies might also work for one of the political parties within a country, to find out the ideas and plans of a rival party. Sometimes spies are even used in the business world, when a company wants to find out what its competitor is doing. (This is called **industrial espionage**.)

WHEN DID SPYING START?

Believe it or not, spies have been at work since the earliest days of recorded history. Check out the Spy Feature on page 44 to find out more!

HOW DO SPIES DO THEIR WORK?

Intelligence officers are trained by the intelligence service they work for. In the United States, the CIA trains its intelligence officers in a secret facility in Virginia known only as "The Farm." In their intelligence training (which happens after college, and sometimes even after graduate school), officers learn the **tradecraft** of the spy world—that is, the special techniques and procedures of espionage. The intelligence officers are then responsible for recruiting and training the secret agents who will do most of the actual spying.

This pen has a secret—it contains a microdot viewer. A microdot is a tiny piece of film that has to be magnified by the viewer in order to be read. When hidden inside a pen, the microdot viewer can be kept in a spy's desk without raising suspicion. This model was used by the KGB (the intelligence service of the former Soviet Union).

The intelligence officer who handles (or manages) a secret agent's work is called the agent's **handler**. The handler gives the agent assignments and "controls" him—kind of like how a chess player controls a pawn. Once an assignment is complete, the handler makes sure that the information collected by the agent gets safely back to headquarters for analysis.

But agents can't always be trusted. Sometimes they become **double agents**, which means they switch their loyalty to an enemy country's intelligence service. They continue working for their original country, hiding the fact that their loyalty has changed! Double agents are *very* dangerous, because they deliberately give their original countries misleading information.

If you think *that's* underhanded, wait till you hear this: Intelligence officers are not always trustworthy, either. Sometimes *they* also secretly work for an enemy intelligence service. When they do that, they're called **moles**. (Imagine a mole burrowing a hole deep into the ground where it lives—get the idea?) Moles can do a *lot* of damage. Not only can they give away the secrets their intelligence service has collected, but they can also blow the covers of the secret agents who work for them. It's a big problem, and a very dangerous one, too.

That's why there are also—get this—**counterspies**. They're officially called **counterintelligence officers**, and their job is to catch moles, double agents, and other enemy spies, and to keep information, equipment, and personnel safe from them. Catching spies is a lot like detective work. (You'll see when you try **Operation Dirty Fingers** on page 32.) In the United States, the FBI (Federal Bureau of Investigation) handles spy catching, among other things.

WHY SPY?

Do you know the saying, "Knowledge is power"? Well, that's the idea. Spying is a way to gain knowledge. It's a sneaky way, though, and it brings up a lot of uneasy questions. We'll talk more about that kind of stuff later. For now, though, even though spying in real life is serious business, think of Spy University as a way of learning the fun stuff: spy secrets, tips, challenges, and games that you can enjoy with other spies-in-training!

spy talk

These are the spy terms your handbook mentions. Study up! And whenever you see a word in **boldface** throughout the book, you can check back here to refresh your memory.

▼ **Agent:** A person who secretly spies for (but is not officially employed by) an intelligence service.

▼ **Base of operations:** A spy's headquarters.

▼ **Biometrics:** The use of unique characteristics, like a fingerprint, to identify a person.

▼ **Cipher:** A form of code in which the letters of a message are replaced with a new set of letters or numbers according to some rule.

▼ **Code:** A system designed to hide the meaning of a message by using letters, numbers, words, symbols, sounds, or signals to represent the actual words of the message.

▼ **Counterintelligence:** The protection of information, people, and equipment from spies.

▼ **Counterspy:** Someone who works in counterintelligence, investigating and catching spies.

▼ **Credential:** An ID card, proving you have security clearance to be inside headquarters.

▼ **Double agent:** A spy who is recruited and controlled by another country's intelligence agency to work secretly against his original agency.

▼ **Escape and evasion:** An area of spy tradecraft that includes all the techniques a spy uses to avoid capture and other dangers.

▼ **Espionage:** The field of spying.

▼ **Handler:** An intelligence officer who manages an agent and gives him assignments.

▼ **Industrial espionage:** Spying in the business world.

▼ **Intelligence:** Another word for the profession of spying, as well as for the information a spy collects.

▼ **Intelligence Officer:** An employee of an intelligence service who recruits the agents who most often do the actual spying.

▼ **Microdot:** A tiny photograph of a document (1mm or smaller) that has to be magnified to be read.

▼ **Microwriting:** Writing that's too small to be read by the naked eye.

▼ **Mole:** An employee of an intelligence service who secretly works for another country's intelligence service.

▼ **Observation post:** A spot from which a spy can conduct surveillance.

▼ **Scouting and reconnaissance:** An area of spy tradecraft that involves obtaining information about the features of a place, or about the location and strength of an enemy army's defenses, for example.

▼ **Secret writing:** The use of invisible inks for undercover communication.

▼ **Spymaster:** The overall head of a spy organization.

▼ **Spy network:** A group of spies who work together toward a common goal.

▼ **Surveillance:** The close study of someone or something (includes watching and listening).

▼ **Tradecraft:** The techniques and procedures that spies use to do their work.

THE CASE OF THE Mysterious BROWN PAPER PACKAGE

It's the first day back at school after a great summer vacation. You're standing outside talking to some friends when a black limo pulls up. Everyone stares in amazement.

A chauffeur jumps out of the driver's seat and opens the back door. Inside the car, you see a man and a boy about your age. The man is handing a package, wrapped in plain brown paper, to the boy. The boy steps out of the car, grabs his backpack, sticks the package into it, and walks toward the school.

"That kid just moved here," someone says. "His name's Jordan, but no one knows much else about him."

"Now *that's* what I call arriving in style," someone else says. "He must be loaded!"

You're puzzled by the new kid, with his limousine entrance and his mysterious package, so you decide to investigate.

■ If you decide to follow Jordan into school right away, turn to **page 36.**

■ If you decide to wait and tail Jordan after school, turn to **page 24**.

OPERATION ID Badge

SPYmissions

Welcome, new Spy University trainee! Glad you're with us! There are just a couple of quick things you'll need to do to get started. First, you'll need to set up a **base of operations**, otherwise known as your spy headquarters. You could call your base "HQ," "The Spy Center," "Home Base," or just "My Room." Whatever you decide, this is your secure area, and you should know who comes and goes, who belongs in and who belongs out, who's on your side and who's not.

That's what a **credential** is good for. On these pages, you can see some examples of credentials from different intelligence agencies. Notice the features these credentials have in common: a picture, some kind of stamp or emblem, a name, and a signature, for starters. They also have designs and stamps that are hard to copy, or else an enemy spy could make a fake credential—and that would be trouble!

Credentials are also used at spy schools. In fact, that's the first thing trainees get when they start at the CIA's school. So, on your first day at Spy University, you're going to make yourself a credential. Later on, you can make more credentials for others in your **spy network**, if you want. But for now, let's start with yours.

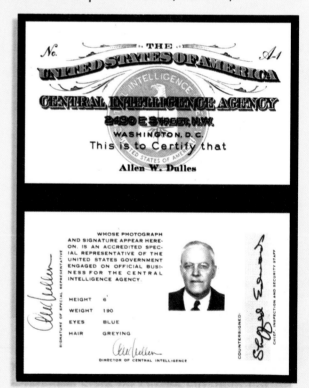

The CIA credential of Allen Dulles, who served as CIA Director from 1953 to 1961.

You're going to make a type of credential called an ID badge. It's a simple credential, just for wearing around headquarters. It's not meant to be worn out in the world. Repeat: *not* out in the world. That's because the purpose of an ID badge is to prove that someone has clearance to be *inside* an intelligence agency's headquarters. It's not meant to broadcast his identity to the world. People who work in intelligence tend to keep their work private, so you should, too. Wear your Spy University ID badge in your HQ, but nowhere else.

A SMERSH credential. SMERSH was the Soviet Union's counter-intelligence service during and just after World War II.

WHAT YOU DO

1 Find a photo of yourself to put on your badge. It's best if the photo has a neutral or white background, but any kind of solid, plain background will do. Small school photos usually work well. The photo should be 1 inch by 1¼ inch (2.5 cm by 3 cm), so measure with the ruler and use the scissors to cut the photo down to size.

2 Use the glue stick to place your photo on your badge.

3 Print your name on your badge, and then sign your name on the line just below it. Your signature is another way to increase security.

If someone else tries to use your badge, he'll have a hard time matching your signature.

4 Go to the Spy University web site (**www.scholastic.com/spy**) to get your trainee number. Once you're at the site, all you have to do is type in your first name and your location—and Spy University headquarters will issue you an official trainee number. Write your number on your badge in the space provided. If you don't have access to the Internet, that's okay. You can just issue yourself a trainee number (any number you want).

13

5 To increase security, you're also going to add your fingerprint. Since no two fingerprints are alike (not even those of identical twins), you will be the only person who will match your badge. To learn how to take your own fingerprints, turn to

thumbprint

Operation Dirty Fingers on page 32. Once you've practiced making your fingerprints, put a print of your right thumb on the back of your badge.

6 Slip your badge into the badge holder, then hang it around your neck. You should wear your badge whenever you're working at headquarters. But remember, when you're out on a mission or

(continued from page 36)

You stay and listen, even though the seconds are ticking down to the bell. You get as close as you can to Jordan and the teacher, but it's still hard to hear what they're saying. You think you hear Jordan say the words "grave" and "after school," but you're not sure. Maybe Jordan's going to a funeral?

You see the teacher write something on her pad of paper, tear the top sheet off, and hand it to Jordan. You realize that an impression of the writing was probably left behind on the pad. You're trying to think of ways you can get to that pad when, to your horror, the bell rings. You're late! You run out of the room. As you go, you think through your options.

- If you decide to go back to the classroom later to see what secrets may have been left behind on the teacher's pad of paper, turn to **page 21**.

- If you decide to go to the graveyard after school, turn to **page 23**.

working undercover, leave your badge at home. You don't want others to know your true identity!

MORE FROM HEADQUARTERS

1 Make ID badges for other members of your spy network. Give each person a role to play. For example, one friend might be in charge of security, making sure that your meetings are secret, while another might be responsible for giving assignments to the spies in the organization. If you go to the Spy University web site (**www.scholastic.com/spy**), you can create and print out more ID badges. You can even create your own spy agency, with its own name and emblem. (You can see some examples of intelligence agency emblems if you turn to page 46.) You can do all this on the Spy University web site, or you can create your own badges by hand.

VISITOR

MY EMBLEM HERE

Visitor's Name

2 Make a visitor ID card. If someone comes to visit your headquarters, she should wear a visitor ID. The visitor ID should have a space for the person's name, your agency emblem, and the word "VISITOR" written clearly across the front. That'll make it clear that the wearer of the badge only has limited security clearance.

WHAT'S THE SECRET?

Remember that a spy needs to make sure he knows who the good guys are! The use of a security credential is the first step.

Besides paper credentials, there are many other ways to make sure that only certain people have access to top secret information. For instance, there's the whole field of **biometrics**. Biometrics uses a person's unique features to identify him or her. For example, using make-up, a person can be made to look like someone else. But it's impossible to use make-up to change a fingerprint or the blood vessel pattern on the inside of the eye. Thumbprint analysis and retinal (eye) scans are two ways that a spy organization can ensure that the person who enters a building or room is who he says he is. Computers can also quickly scan a person's face, analyze his voice, and compare his signature to the one that's on record! Now you know why you signed and fingerprinted your card!

(continued from page 24)

Y ou dash into Ed's Hardware and tell the cashier you're looking for the boy who just left in the truck.

"You mean Ed's nephew?" asks the cashier. "Jordan?"

"Yes," you say. "Do you know where they went?"

"I don't know. Ed just said he'd be back in a second," the cashier said with a shrug.

Deciding to press your luck, you ask, "Do you happen to know what was in that brown paper package that Jordan brought in here?"

"I have no idea," the cashier says, looking at you like you're way too nosy.

■ Nice try, but that was a dead end! Turn back to **page 11** and start over!

The red-and-white striped border of your ID badge is a special security feature. This border is used in the spy world on top secret documents. That way, everyone knows to be extra careful with them (and not leave them lying around in the open, or among other papers on a desk). So, let the stripes remind you to keep your ID badge safe and sound!

Can you spot the top secret document?

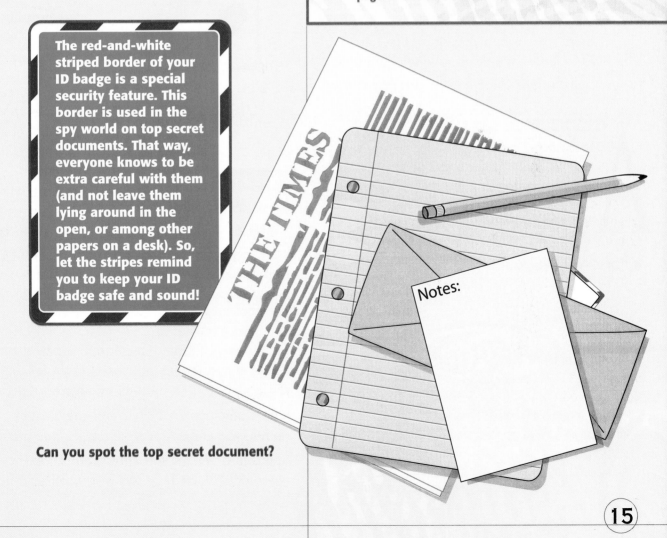

#2 OPERATION Motion NOTION

S o, you've got your spy headquarters up and running, but are you sure that it's secure? What if someone tries to sneak in while you're having a secret meeting? Will you know right away? You *will* if you have your trusty Spy Guard motion detector on the watch! Your Spy Guard can also be placed inside a bag, on top of a notebook, inside a drawer, or anywhere you have something you want to protect from snoopers. It looks like an innocent key chain, so you'll really catch those sneaks by surprise! Your Spy Guard even has a silent mode, so you can tell if your stuff was touched while you were gone (and the snooper will be none the wiser!). Amazing!

STUFF YOU'LL NEED
- **Spy Guard motion detector**
- **Notebook**

WHAT YOU DO

First, get your Spy Guard into disguise! Attach a key to it, so no one will suspect its true function. Then try the next three activities to get an idea of what your Spy Guard can do.

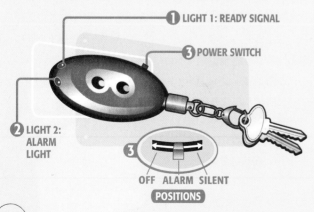

1 LIGHT 1: READY SIGNAL

3 POWER SWITCH

2 LIGHT 2: ALARM LIGHT

3 OFF ALARM SILENT
POSITIONS

PART 1: KEEP OFF!

You want to make sure your notebook with your secret notes is safe while you step away from your desk for a moment. What can you do?

1 Place your notebook on top of your desk. Put the Spy Guard on top of the notebook.

2 Put the Spy Guard in alarm mode by sliding the switch to the alarm position. Wait for the ready light to flash three times, and then the alarm is armed and ready.

3 If anyone tries to pick up the notebook, the Spy Guard will let you know with a loud alarm. The alarm light will also flash, and it will continue to flash after the alarm sound stops. That way, if you're gone too long or too far to hear the alarm, you can still tell if the notebook was moved.

PART 2:
INTRUDER ALERT!

You're in a secret meeting at your headquarters and you want to make sure that no unauthorized people sneak in. What can you do?

1 Close the door to your headquarters.

2 Place the Spy Guard on the floor in front of the door. Make sure that the door will tap the Spy Guard when it opens. If necessary, place the device on top of a book.

3 Put the Spy Guard in alarm mode. After three seconds, the unit is armed and ready.

4 If anyone tries to open the door, the Spy Guard will sound the alarm. Try it and see what happens!

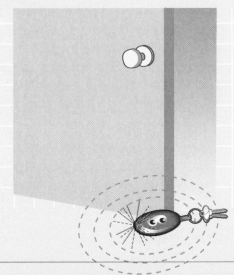

PART 3:
WHILE YOU WERE OUT...

You suspect that someone's been reading your notebook while you're not around, but you aren't sure. You want to be confident that your secrets are safe. What do you do? Use your Spy Guard's silent mode! In silent mode, the alarm won't sound when the Spy Guard is moved. Instead, only the alarm light will turn on.

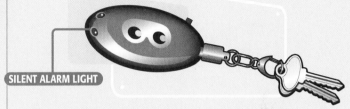

SILENT ALARM LIGHT

1 Place the Spy Guard on top of your notebook. Make sure that you can see the signal lights without having to move the device. (You don't want to set off the motion detector yourself when you come back to check it later!)

2 Put the Spy Guard in silent mode by sliding the switch to the silent position. Give it three seconds to get ready.

3 Leave your notebook alone. When you come back, check the report from your Spy Guard. If the alarm light is blinking, then the notebook was moved while you were gone. That means you've probably caught a snooper! But before you panic, make sure there's no other way the Spy Guard could have been set off (you know, like by your cat climbing on top of your desk or something).

MORE FROM HEADQUARTERS

1 Put the Spy Guard inside your backpack or dresser drawer, making sure that it sits in a horizontal position. Turn on the alarm mode (not the silent mode). If a snooper comes prying, you'll hear about it!

2 Use the Spy Guard's instant alarm. Just pull out the keys whenever you need to send a signal, and the alarm will sound immediately.

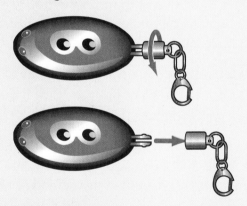

3 Detach the key ring to use your Spy Guard without its disguise.

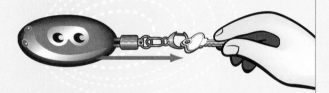

WHAT'S THE SECRET?

The Spy Guard's alarm sounds when it's moved because of the way electricity is controlled inside it. To quickly explain, electricity is a form of energy caused by the movement of tiny particles called electrons. In order for electrons to move, two things are needed: electrical energy (which comes from the Spy Guard's battery) and a complete electric circuit. A complete electric circuit means that there's a complete circular path for the electrons to take to and from the battery. The Spy Guard's alarm has a circuit that goes from the battery, through wires to the alarm, and back through other wires to the opposite end of the battery.

However—and this is a big however—the alarm circuit *also* has a very sensitive switch that only gets turned on when the Spy Guard is moved. That switch completes the circuit, meaning that electricity flows into the alarm and turns it on. And you've *heard* what happens then!

This motion detector was used by the KGB (the intelligence service of the former Soviet Union). It used infrared light beams to sense motion, and it was connected to a camera that snapped a picture of the snooper!

SPYquest

(continued from page 36)

You sneakily walk up to Jordan's desk. As you reach for the notebook, you notice that Jordan has left his keys on top. You start to slide the keys aside, but all of a sudden, a horrible siren starts blaring from the key chain. A motion detector! You should have known! Jordan and the teacher quickly turn around, eyes wide. The room goes silent. You've been caught!

"What's going on here?" the teacher asks, looking very concerned. Jordan looks pretty suspicious and kind of mad, too. You say it was an accident and run out of the room.

■ That was definitely a dead end! Turn back to **page 11** and try again!

#3 OPERATION surveillance Star!

Surveillance is the careful study of a person or a place. It's a key part of a spy's work, and it's all about careful observation. Sometimes a spy will have only a quick glance at a document or a short visit to a secret building, and he'll have to notice and remember lots of important details. This takes keen eyes and a sharp memory. So, to hone your skills of observation, try this activity. See if you can achieve surveillance stardom!

WHAT YOU DO

PART 1: EYE SPY

1 Look at the picture on this page for thirty seconds. Try to remember as many of the items in this scene as you can.

2 After thirty seconds, close the book and list all the things you remember on a sheet of paper.

3 Open up the book and compare your answers to the picture. Then rate yourself using the chart above. How observant were you?

PART 2:
WHAT'S CHANGED?

1 Look back at the picture on page 19. Give yourself thirty seconds to remember the details.

2 Now look at the picture below. There are fifteen changes from the original picture on page 19. Can you spot them?

3 On your piece of paper, write down as many of the changes as you can find.

4 Check your answers on page 48. If you found ten or more changes, then you're a surveillance star!

MORE FROM HEADQUARTERS

1 Cover the picture on page 20 and see if you can answer some questions from what you remember. (Check your answers on page 48.)

   a. What sport does this person play?
   b. What kind of pet does this person have?
   c. Where is this person thinking of traveling?

2 Wait a day, and without looking at the first picture again, make another list of all the items you still remember from it. How good is your memory of the scene now?

WHAT'S THE SECRET?

When you observe something, whether it's a picture in a book or an actual scene in real life, you create images in your mind. Light reflects off the paper or the scene and travels through the lenses of your eye to the retina, where the images are transformed into a series of electrical signals. These signals are then transmitted to your brain and stored until you need to remember them later.

As you discovered in this activity, there's a lot of room for error in this process, because you can't pay attention to *all* the signals that your eyes take in. You have to be selective and focus on certain ones. That's why you might not have noticed certain details when you first looked at the picture. Or maybe you saw the details but didn't think they were important enough to make a point of remembering.

If you did the second **More from Headquarters** activity, you also learned that time affects memory. Much of what you observe is stored in your short-term memory, and you only remember it for a few hours, or maybe even just a few minutes. If you store observations in your long-term memory, however, you may remember

them for years. Repeating something over and over can help you remember.

You can improve your powers of observation with practice. For example, look at a picture in a magazine for thirty seconds, and then close the magazine and write down everything that you saw. Compare your notes with the real thing and write down the items that you left out. Keep practicing, and you'll get better and better!

(continued from page 14)

Since no one is in the classroom when you stop by after school, you have easy access to the pad on the teacher's desk. You rip off the top sheet and lightly shade over it with your pencil. This is what you reveal:

- If you decide to go to 224 Boswell Street at 4:00 p.m., turn to **page 42**.

- If you decide you'd be better off searching through the trash can for the paper you saw Jordan throw out that morning, turn to **page 43**.

224 Boswell Street!!
4:00 p.m.

OPERATION SLY CAMERA

What would spies do without cameras? Cameras are among the most important tools of **espionage**. They're used to photograph people, places, events, and things (usually documents). They're very important in **surveillance** and in another tradecraft area called **scouting and reconnaissance** (that is, collecting information about the features of a place, or about an enemy army's strengths and weaknesses, for example). In both cases, the camera creates a record of what the spy saw, so it can be carefully examined later.

Spies usually need to take photos secretly, or else they'll attract a lot of attention and make people suspicious. But how can someone take a photo without being noticed?

STUFF YOU'LL NEED

- **Camera with film inside***
- **Newspaper**
- **Pencil**
- **Scissors**
- **Double-sided tape**

* **Note:** If you don't have your own camera, ask a senior spy (an adult in your family) if you can borrow one. A small camera is better than a large one for spy work, so see what you can dig up. If you can't use a family camera, you can purchase a small, disposable camera for this activity.

CAMERA

Lever to adjust camera for different light conditions

Hidden camera in a book.

LENS OPENING

Hidden cameras in a watch and a lipstick case. The lipstick camera was used to photograph documents.

LENS OPENING

LIPSTICK

TOP OF LIPSTICK CASE

CAMERA BODY

BOTTOM OF LIPSTICK CASE

LENS OPENING

Spies have lots of ways! They hide little cameras in neckties, wristwatches, pens, umbrellas—you name it! Check out the pictures on these pages for some examples. Then try the following activity to learn how to use a camera in sly spy mode!

WHAT YOU DO

1 Make sure your camera is loaded with film and ready to go. Ask a senior spy for help if you need it.

SHUTTER BUTTON

LENS

VIEWFINDER

2 Find a section of the newspaper that you can cut a hole in. (That is, make sure no one wants to read it later!) The newspaper should be folded in half, like newspapers usually are.

3 Place the newspaper on a table with the front page headlines facing down. Then lift the top half of the paper and place the camera inside the fold, near the right side, with the lens pointing

away from you. You should still be able to reach the camera's shutter button when you hold the paper by the sides.

4 Using your pencil, mark the paper in front of the camera's lens.

5 Remove the camera, and cut a hole with your scissors all the way through the newspaper. Make the hole the same size as the camera's lens.

6 Put a small piece of double-sided tape on either side of the hole.

(continued from page 14)

The graveyard's a pretty quiet and lonely place after school. Kind of spooky, too. So what are you doing here? This is a dead end!

■ Turn back to **page 11** and start again.

7 Place the camera on the newspaper so that the lens is right over the hole. Press the camera into the tape. The tape will hold the camera in place so the lens will always be aligned with the hole.

8 Fold the newspaper with the camera inside. Lift the newspaper by the sides, with your right index finger inside the fold, ready to press the camera's shutter button.

9 Now, go outside, have a seat, and pretend you're reading something on the front page of the newspaper. Pick something to photograph, like your house, a mailbox, or a car. Adjust the position of the newspaper so that the camera is pointing in the right direction and click the shutter to take your picture. Very sly!

HIDDEN CAMERA

MORE FROM HEADQUARTERS

Ask a friend if you can take a picture of him the next day. Tell him he won't know when the photo will be taken, but challenge him to guess. Hide the camera in the newspaper, and see if you can take his picture without him noticing!

A word to wise spies: Since you're just *practicing* undercover photography, always ask people's permission *before* you take their pictures. Some people are sensitive about that kind of thing!

WHAT'S THE SECRET?

A newspaper is a good place to hide a camera because it's an ordinary object. People sit outside reading newspapers all the time, so there's no reason for this to attract suspicion. What other everyday objects might be good for hiding cameras? Use your imagination!

SPYquest

(continued from page 11)

At the end of the day, you follow Jordan out the school doors. Jumping on your bike, you stay a short distance behind him as he walks up the street, toward the center of town. Jordan stops in two different stores—a card store and an office supply store—and you wait for him outside each one. Finally, he goes into a small neighborhood store called Ed's Hardware. You peek into the window and see Jordan handing his small brown paper package to the man behind the counter. Then Jordan steps behind the counter, too. A few minutes later, both Jordan and the man walk out of the store, get into a truck that says Ed's Hardware, and drive away.

■ If you decide to follow the truck on your bike, turn to **page 34**.

■ If you decide to ask the cashier at Ed's Hardware what was going on, turn to **page 15**.

5

TRADECRAFT AREA

Surveillance

OPERATION LOOKOUT

One way of conducting **surveillance** is to set up an **observation post** (sometimes called an "O.P." for short). There are lots of reasons why a spy does this. Maybe he suspects someone's following him, so he needs to keep watch on his headquarters to make sure no one suspicious is lurking around. Or maybe the spy has been assigned to keep someone under surveillance, and that person often goes jogging in a certain park. The spy might want to keep watch on the park, to see what's going on there. Both of these situations call for an observation post. There are two different kinds of O.P.'s— fixed and mobile—and in this activity, you'll learn how to set up both of them. So grab your Telemicro, and let's have a look!

STUFF YOU'LL NEED

- Telemicro
- Notebook
- Pencil

YOUR NETWORK

A friend you can observe

WHAT YOU DO

PART 1: THE FIXED OBSERVATION POST

A fixed observation post is a stationary place where a spy can conduct surveillance. The spy may stay at the fixed observation post for hours or even days at a time, or the post may be a place that the spy returns to on a regular basis (at a certain time each day, for example). The spy will keep a record of what he sees, called a "surveillance log." So, choose a place you want to observe (like your front yard, the sidewalk in front of your house, or anywhere else that's safe and interests you), and follow these steps to set up your own fixed observation post.

1 Choose a spot (like your bedroom window) where you have the best view of the area you want to observe. Make sure that you can watch from this place without being seen.

2 Choose a time that you will go to your observation post. For example, you could plan to be at your post from 11:00 to 11:20 every Saturday morning.

3 Now, set yourself up in your O.P. with your Telemicro and your notebook, and observe! In your notebook, keep your surveillance log, recording everything you

Surveillance Log

11:01: Dark-haired boy rides by on bike

11:04: Old lady walks by with poodle

11:13 Mail delivery

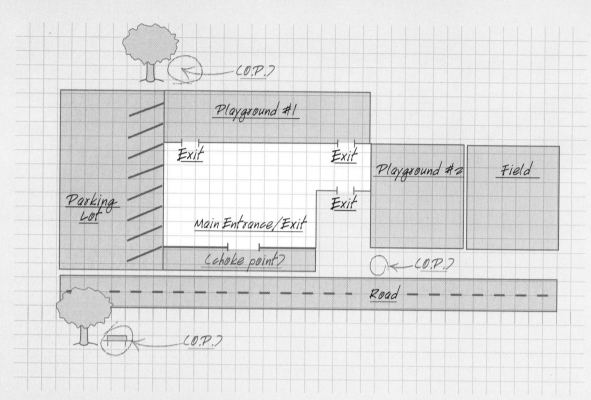

see and the time you see it. Use your Telemicro to get a closer look whenever you need to.

4 Draw some conclusions from your observation. For example, does the lady next door walk her dog at the same time every day? Is there anything that seems strange? For example, is there a delivery to a neighbor at an unusual time?

PART 2: THE MOBILE OBSERVATION POST

Unlike a fixed O.P., a mobile observation post can change location. Spies use mobile O.P.'s when they have to keep track of a person who's moving. They'll watch from one place, and then when the person they're watching (who's called the "target" of their surveillance) moves out of range, they'll move their observation post. Follow these steps to learn how spies think their mobile O.P.'s through.

1 Choose a place you know, like your school or a local park.

2 Draw a map of the area, showing all entrances and exits. Now, if you had to observe someone who went to this location every day, where would you watch from? Mark the locations of several possible observation posts. Which locations allow you to see the most? And which locations allow you to watch without being seen?

3 Is there a place (like a main exit) where everyone passes through? This kind of spot is called a "choke point." Look for choke points, and label them on your map. That's where you'll see the most action. Choke points are a good place to start your surveillance, so you can catch your target going into (or coming out of) the location.

4 Now you need to decide how you'll move when it comes time to change your location to keep your target in view. Will you observe on foot, or do you think you might need to have a bike on hand? How much distance will you be able to cover?

5 What other equipment will you need? Your Telemicro will allow you to see things up close, but what else might you want to have on hand? Remember, you're on the move, so you'll need to travel lightly.

6 What will you wear, so you don't attract a lot of attention?

7 Phew, that was a lot of planning! But those are the kinds of questions that help spies prepare for a surveillance operation. You're all set to give it a try—but one word of advice first: *Never* make eye contact with your target! That's the key to watching without being seen.

MORE FROM HEADQUARTERS

1 Use your Telemicro to see if you can read license plate numbers on a car from different distances. How far away can you be and still read the numbers? If your surveillance target were to get picked up by a car, you'd need this information!

2 Ask a friend to keep watch on you from an observation post that you know about. Can you see him as he watches you? What things do you notice that draw attention to him? Use this information to help improve your own observation post so you can avoid attracting unwanted attention.

WHAT'S THE SECRET?

The telescope in your Telemicro uses two lenses to magnify the image of the person or thing you're looking at. This makes distant objects seems closer than they really are. You can find out more about lenses on page 31.

SPYtales

If you added a telescope to the front end of a camera, you could take pictures from a long distance away, even from outer space! A camera in an airplane or satellite can carry out surveillance of any part of enemy territory that lies beneath its flight path or orbit. The photos can then be analyzed, and buildings, factories, bridges, weapons, and other enemy equipment can be counted and evaluated.

In 1956, the United States introduced the U-2 spy plane, which it sent on flights over the Soviet Union. The U-2 flew at such a high altitude (about twice as high as commercial flights) that it was out of range of Soviet aircraft and missiles of the time. It took photos of the build-up of Soviet nuclear weapons, providing valuable information to the United States.

Spy planes also took high altitude photos of Cuba in 1962. On close inspection of the photos, it was learned that the Soviet Union was placing nuclear missiles in Cuba (right off the coast of Florida!). This information led the United States to react by placing an embargo on Cuba, preventing supplies from going into or out of the island, until the Soviet Union removed its missiles.

The missiles were removed a short time later, but only after a terrifying thirteen-day ordeal—called the Cuban Missile Crisis—when the world was at the brink of nuclear war.

OPERATION invisible INK

Here's a great technique that lets spies hide their messages: Invisible ink! This is also called **secret writing** or "SW" for short, and it's one way to ensure that a secret message being sent back to headquarters is kept safely undercover. There are lots of easy ways to make invisible ink. Try this one, and you'll be able to hide some really *juicy* messages!

STUFF YOU'LL NEED

- **One or two lemons, sliced in half (with an adult's help)**
- **Small bowl**
- **Cotton swab**
- **Sheet of white paper**
- **Ballpoint pen**
- **Lamp**

YOUR NETWORK

A friend to receive your message

WHAT YOU DO

1 Squeeze the lemon halves into the bowl. You should end up with about ¼ cup (65 ml) of lemon juice.

2 Dip the cotton swab into the lemon juice and write your secret message on the sheet of white paper. Maybe it's something like, "Meet in the park at noon."

3 Allow the message to dry. You shouldn't be able to see the message after it has dried, so your piece of paper should still look blank.

4 A blank white piece of paper isn't a normal thing to send to your friend, though, is it? That would look very suspicious! So, using your ballpoint pen, write another message on the other side of the paper, like a regular old note to a friend. Make it innocent, so no one will suspect anything!

5 Secretly pass the note to your friend.

6 Your friend will turn on the lamp and hold the "blank" side of the paper close to the lightbulb.

7 After a few minutes, your friend will be able to read your secret message!

MORE FROM HEADQUARTERS

1 Try writing invisible messages with other liquids like grapefruit juice or vinegar, and see which ones work best for you.

2 Try developing the message in other ways. For example, have an adult help you hold the secret message over the heat from a toaster. Is this a better way to develop the secret writing? Worse?

3 Try writing the invisible message between the lines of a note you've already written. Or, you can write the invisible message in the margins of your note. You can even try writing the note on the edge of a newspaper!

WHAT'S THE SECRET?

Fruit juices and many other liquids, like milk and soda, contain the element carbon. When carbon is dissolved in some liquids (like lemon juice), it looks clear. However, when the liquid

(continued from page 43)

It's Sunday—what a great day to be at the park! But where's Jordan? Nowhere in sight, that's where! Something definitely went wrong with your decoding and you've hit a dead end.

■ Turn back to **page 11** and start again.

SPYtales

When U.S. military intelligence intercepted a letter written in secret ink to a suspected German spy during World War I, they traced the letter back to Madame Marie de Victorica, in New York. When they arrested her in 1918, she had two silk scarves that were covered with invisible ink! She never went on trial because she offered to work for the U.S. government.

is heated, a chemical reaction occurs, and the carbon shows its true colors: dark brown or black. This is why the lemon juice turns brown when heated. (By the way, carbon also appears when you cook a piece of toast, which is why toast turns dark brown—or black when you burn it.)

This handkerchief has a secret message that was written in West Germany in the 1960s. It mentions a meeting that was about to take place and some information that was going to arrive from East Germany. The message was revealed by applying a chemical to the handkerchief.

TRADECRAFT AREA

Undercover communications

Invisible ink is not the only way that spies can hide words. Messages can also be made so tiny that you can't read them with the naked eye. This is called **microwriting**. Real microwriting is so small that it can't even be read with a magnifier like the one in your Telemicro device. You'd need a lot stronger magnification! Check out the pictures on this page, and you can see where real microwriting has been hidden. Then try this activity and discover the power of thinking small!

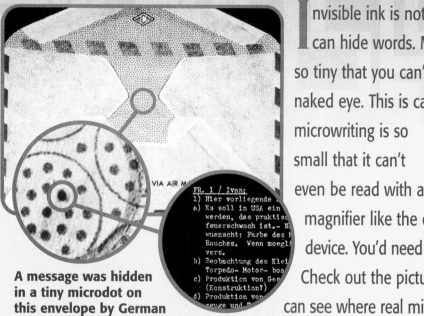

FR. 1 / Ivan:
1) Hier vorliegende
a) Es soll in USA ein
   werden, das praktis
   feuerschwach ist.- N
   wuenscht: Farbe des
   Rauches. Wenn moegli
   vers.
b) Beobachtung des Klei
   Torpedo- Motor- boa
c) Produktion von Ge
   (Konstruktion?)
d) Produktion von
   zeuge und

A message was hidden in a tiny microdot on this envelope by German military intelligence during World War II.

STUFF YOU'LL NEED
- **Telemicro**

This fake tear-out page was created for an American spy's copy of *National Geographic* magazine. There is a tiny message (in a number code) engraved in one of the lines. This allowed the spy to keep the information secretly in his apartment in Moscow.

WHAT YOU DO

1 Scan the postcard pictures on page 31 and see if you can identify some areas where microwriting might be hidden.

2 Now take out your Telemicro, pull out the top part, and look through the hollow bottom tube to magnify parts of the pictures where you think

26173 67352 78630 87463 45628 11354 32986 45098 67207 89023 59827 64092 16492 56398 34592
38175 87493 15382 59375 09217 36250 06899 28462 69326 92475 83204 09362 28462 57398 29846

Can you find the hidden microwriting?

microwriting is hidden. When you think you see letters, hold the Telemicro close to the paper and then slowly move it away. What happens to the size of the letters?

USE THIS MAGNIFIER

3 You should find a message in each picture. Check your answers on page 48.

MORE FROM HEADQUARTERS

Go to the Spy University web site at **www.scholastic.com/spy** and scan pictures with hidden microwriting!

WHAT'S THE SECRET?

The Telemicro's magnifier (or microscope) works because of its lens. A lens is a curved piece of glass or plastic that bends rays of light that pass through it.

Rays of light come from everything you look at, including the page you're reading now. When you look through a lens, though, you're seeing *bent* light rays, and they can make the object

seem bigger. That's what happens when you look at the little letters through the lens of your Telemicro. That's also what happens when you wear a pair of glasses!

If you want to magnify things even more, look through two lenses at once. That's how powerful microscopes are designed.

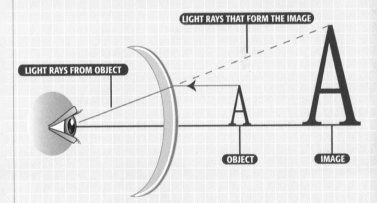

LIGHT RAYS THAT FORM THE IMAGE

LIGHT RAYS FROM OBJECT

OBJECT

IMAGE

SPYquest

(continued from page 34)

This time, the truck speeds off into the distance. You're tired now, and you can't keep up, so it's a dead end for you. Better luck next time!

■ Turn back to **page 11** to start over.

Fingerprinting is a very important tool for **counterspies**. Suppose, for example, that some enemy spy has stolen the designs for a new airplane from a safe in a factory. Just like detectives, counterspies may be able to use fingerprints left at the scene to identify the spy (since, as you learned in **Operation ID Badge**, fingerprints are a form of **biometric** identification). So, here's a little introduction to the basics of fingerprinting. See if you can use these techniques to catch a spy!

STUFF YOU'LL NEED

- 👓 **Telemicro**
- 👓 **Fingerprint cards**
- **Pen**
- **Pencil**
- **Clear tape**
- **Several sheets of plain white paper**

YOUR NETWORK

Three enemy agents (that is, friends to fingerprint)

WHAT YOU DO

PART 1: MAKE YOUR OWN FINGERPRINT RECORD

1 Before you start, look at your fingertips using your Telemicro's magnifier. Can you see the lines and grooves on the tip of each finger? That's what makes your fingerprints.

2 Now, let's make a fingerprint record for you. Begin by filling in your name at the top of one of your fingerprint cards.

3 Next, make a copy of each fingerprint. To do this, make a square of pencil dust on a sheet of paper by rubbing the pencil point back and forth many times.

4 Press your right thumb on the black square and roll it back and forth until the tip of your thumb is covered with pencil dust.

5 Tear off a piece of tape about 2 inches (5 cm) long. Press the sticky side of the tape onto your right thumb.

6 Peel off the tape and stick it on the right thumb square of your fingerprint card.

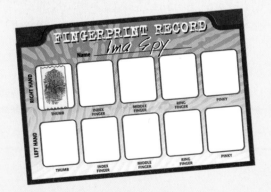

FINGERPRINT RECORD
Name *Ima Spy*

	THUMB	INDEX FINGER	MIDDLE FINGER	RING FINGER	PINKY
RIGHT HAND					
LEFT HAND					

7 You may need to rub the pencil point on the paper again to get more dust for the next fingerprint. Once you have enough dust, repeat steps 4 through 6 with your right index finger. Then move on to your middle, ring, and pinky fingers until you have a complete set of prints for your right hand.

8 Repeat steps 4 through 7 with your left hand. Do you notice the differences between the fingerprints from each hand? That's why it's important to get all ten prints!

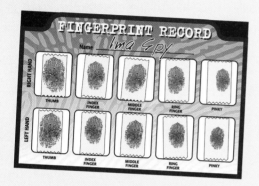

9 Wash your hands so you don't leave fingerprints everywhere!

10 Now that you have your fingerprints, use your Telemicro's magnifier to examine them. Which of these fingerprint types looks like yours?

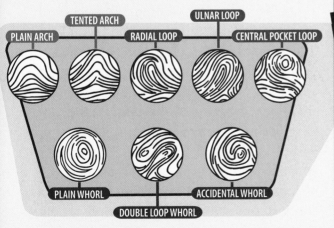

1 Create fingerprint records for three of your friends. We'll call them enemy agents! Use one card for each enemy agent, and follow the steps from Part 1.

2 Collect the fingerprint records from each of the enemy agents.

3 Now have your enemy agents make a single fingerprint (their choice) on a separate piece of paper. Tell them to label these papers with a secret mark that only they will know. When they're done, have them turn their papers over.

4 Collect the papers and mix them up.

5 Choose one of the papers at random. Now's the fun part. Pretend this is a fingerprint from the spy who stole the designs for the new airplane from the safe in the factory—you know, the one from the introduction to this operation. Which one of your enemy agents did the deed?

6 Use your Telemicro's magnifier to compare the single fingerprint to those on your enemy agents' fingerprint records. Can you discover who stole the designs? Use the secret mark to see if you're right!

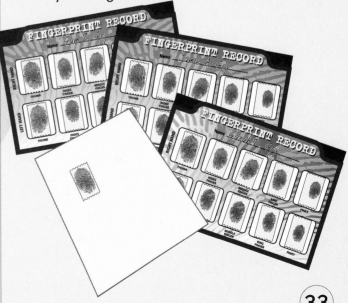

MORE FROM HEADQUARTERS

What can you do to make comparing finger-prints easier? Begin by describing a main feature of each fingerprint. Does it have an arch, a loop, or a whorl? Look at the picture of the fingerprint types on page 33 if you're not sure. If you were looking for a fingerprint with an arch, you'd only have to compare it to others with an arch, and not ones with a loop or whorl. That would help narrow down your search a lot.

Which fingerprint type is this?

(continued from page 24)

You follow the truck on your bike, using the bike path beside the road. It's a good thing it's a big truck, because otherwise it would be hard to keep it in view. Sometimes it gets far ahead of you, but because of the traffic lights, you're able to keep up. Soon you see the truck turning into the parking lot of one of your favorite parks, Cold Creek Park. You're just about to follow the truck when you see a group of your friends on their way out of the park. They're going to have pizza at someone's house, and they lean on you to join them. It's very tempting (especially since you're hungry), but you know what you have to do. You're just about to make your excuses when you see the truck leaving the park.

- ■ If you decide to follow the truck, turn to **page 31**.
- ■ If you decide to see if Jordan was dropped off at the park, turn to **page 39**.

SPYtales

During World War I, Alfred Redl, the chief of Austrian military counterintelligence, used a clever technique to get fingerprints from people who visited his office. He had his office arranged so that a glossy cigarette case was within reach of the visitor. Then, when Redl offered the visitor a cigarette, the visitor would help himself, leaving his finger-prints behind on the case. This helped identify who the visitor really was, since spies often used false identities. The East German STASI (secret police) used a similar technique—they would offer the visitor a glass of water and take finger-prints from the glass. The STASI also collected saliva samples and worked to capture and preserve people's scents as well!

WHAT'S THE SECRET?

The skin on the tips of your fingers is covered with tiny ridges called friction ridges. These ridges create friction and allow you to pick up things more easily. Fingerprints are made because the glands in your hands secrete liquids, mainly sweat and oils. When you touch a flat surface, some of these liquids are left behind in a pattern that's the same as your fingertip ridges. Since everyone has a unique set of these ridges, a fingerprint found at the scene of a theft can be used to identify the criminal.

Did you figure out who the spy was? You probably had a difficult time. It's really hard to compare fingerprints with the human eye! That's why it isn't done that way anymore. Now, computers scan a fingerprint and compare it to huge files that have been collected from intelligence agencies and crime-fighting organizations around the world. This computer system, called AFIS (Automatic Fingerprint Identification System), can compare an unknown fingerprint to millions of others in the system in a fraction of a second. It only works, though, if the person you're searching for is in the database.

OPERATION Shady GROOVES

As you learned in **Operation Invisible Ink**, blank paper is not always as blank as it looks. It can be a keeper of secrets, and a good **counterspy** (spy catcher) knows how to coax those secrets out. It's simple: If a spy is writing on a pad of paper (or a stack of paper), the pressure of his pen is not just felt by the sheet he's writing on—the sheet underneath feels it, too. The writing leaves grooves on the lower sheet, and it's not hard for an artful counterspy to *draw* those hidden words out!

STUFF YOU'LL NEED

- **Pad (or a small stack) of blank white paper**
- **Ballpoint pen**
- **Pencil**

YOUR NETWORK

A friend to write the secret message that you'll expose

WHAT YOU DO

1 First, try the method yourself. Use the ballpoint pen to write your name on the top sheet of paper.

2 Remove the top sheet and you should be able to see some faint grooves on the sheet underneath.

3 With your pencil, lightly shade over the faint grooves. There's your name. Groovy!

4 Now that you know the drill, give your pad to a friend and have him write you a message and tear off the top sheet.

5 Use the shading technique to reveal the message on the sheet underneath! Check with your friend to see if you got it right.

MORE FROM HEADQUARTERS

1 Play a shady game of hide-and-seek. Have your friend write the location of his hiding place on the pad, rip off the top sheet, and go hide. Can you find your friend just by using the evidence you uncover on the sheet underneath?

2 Pass engraved notes! To everyone else, they'll look like blank paper, so your secrets will be safe from unwelcome eyes!

3 Try shading the paper that's *two* sheets below the one you wrote on. Can you still pick up the writing? Try a page lower. How low can you go and still see the writing?

WHAT'S THE SECRET?

Paper's soft, so it easily caves in under pressure. You'll get the deepest grooves if you use thin paper (with a hard surface underneath) and press hard with your pen.

The method you learned for revealing this writing is known in the spy world as "the detection of indented writing."

Counterspies have lots of different ways of revealing indented writing. In a special technique called Electro-static Detection, a piece of paper is covered in cellophane and charged with static electricity. When toner dust (like the kind used in copy machines) is sprinkled over the paper, indented writing can be picked up four pages (or more) below the original writing!

(continued from page 11)

You still have five minutes before school starts, so you follow Jordan down the hallway to his classroom. Since it's the first day of school, you can sneak into his class without being noticed. He takes a seat right in the front row, even though most of the other kids are hanging around the back of the room, talking and laughing. He immediately pulls a notebook out of his huge backpack, flips to a back page, and starts studying it very seriously. Whoa, you think. This guy doesn't play around!

You walk by Jordan's desk and sneak a peek at his notebook. You're shocked to see that it's full of rows and rows of crazy letters that don't spell any words! You walk by again,

just to double-check, and sure enough, it looks like nonsense. Could this kid be writing in another language?

As you watch, Jordan tears out a page from his notebook, crumbles it up into a ball, and tosses it into the trash can at the front of the room. Hmmm…You start to wonder if there's a way you can reach into that trash can without looking too weird or suspicious.

But then something better happens: Jordan gets up from his seat and goes up to talk to the teacher. You quickly move closer so you can listen. You struggle to hear what he's saying, though, since more and more kids are entering the room and the noise level is getting

higher. Time is not on your side, either, since you only have a minute to get to your class or you'll be late on the first day of school! That would definitely be a bad start to the year! But still, you're tempted to stay and listen—and you also notice that Jordan has left his notebook unattended on his desk.

- If you decide to peek into Jordan's notebook, turn to **page 18**.

- If you decide to come back and investigate the trash later, turn to **page 43**.

- If you decide to risk being late to class so you can listen in on Jordan's conversation with his teacher, turn to **page 14**.

OPERATION SPY time

W e all know how important it is to get to places on time, whether you're going to school, to the movies, to the airport, to the dentist (ugh), or to somebody's surprise party (yeah!). If you're late, things can get messy. Being on time is very important to spies, too. They may need to be at a secret meeting at a specific time; they may need to know what time an operation in another part of the world will begin, or they may need to be at the designated escape point just in time to be whisked away to safety! But how do spies ensure that there are no mistakes in timing, even if they communicate over thousands of miles and across many different time zones? Try these activities to see how the use of military time and Greenwich Mean Time keeps spies around the world working on the same clock.

STUFF YOU'LL NEED

- **Pencil and paper**
- **A watch or clock**

WHAT YOU DO

PART 1: MILITARY TIME

Spies prefer military time, which uses a 24-hour clock instead of a.m. and p.m. That way, there's less room for confusion. You can imagine what a disaster it would be if you thought an operation started at 7:00 a.m. when it was really supposed to start at 7:00 p.m.! So, let's make a military time log of your activities for one day. Pick any day you want, but today or yesterday are probably freshest in your mind.

1 On a piece of paper, make a chart with three columns. Label them, from left to right, <u>Time</u>, <u>Military Time</u>, and <u>Activity</u>.

2 In the Activity column on the right side, list all your activities for the day, starting when you woke up and ending when you went to sleep.

3 In the Time column, write the times of all your activities in regular old 12-hour (that's a.m. and p.m.) time.

Time	Military time	Activity
1:00 a.m.	01:00 hours	wake up
1:15 a.m.	01:15 hours	wash up & get dressed
1:30 a.m.	01:30 hours	breakfast
1:40 a.m.	01:40 hours	leave for school
8:00 a.m.	08:00 hours	arrive at school
11:30 a.m.	11:30 hours	lunch
2:20 p.m.	14:20 hours	leave school
2:40 p.m.	14:40 hours	arrive home
3:00 p.m.	15:00 hours	walk dog
6:30 p.m.	18:30 hours	eat dinner

37

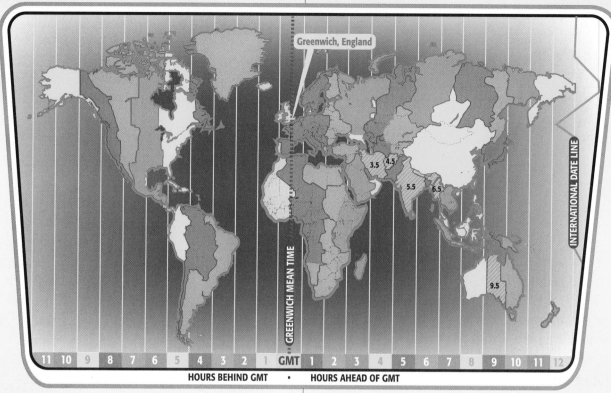

Greenwich, England

INTERNATIONAL DATE LINE

3.5   4.5

5.5   6.5

9.5

GREENWICH MEAN TIME

| 11 | 10 | 9 | 8 | 7 | 6 | 5 | 4 | 3 | 2 | 1 | GMT | 1 | 2 | 3 | 4 | 5 | 6 | 7 | 8 | 9 | 10 | 11 | 12 |

HOURS BEHIND GMT • HOURS AHEAD OF GMT

4 Fill in the Military Time column for the morning. In military time, the a.m. hours stay the same, but numbers less than ten are given a zero in front of them. For example, 7:00 a.m. becomes 07:00 military time (pronounced oh seven hundred hours). 12:00 noon is easy, just 12:00 military time, so no worries there.

5 Now fill in the military times for the afternoon and evening. In military time, the p.m. hours all have twelve added to them, completing the 24-hour clock. For example, 1:00 p.m. is 13:00 in military time (pronounced thirteen hundred hours), and 9:30 p.m. becomes 21:30 in military time (pronounced twenty-one thirty). Midnight is 24:00 in military time (twenty-four hundred hours) or, sometimes, 0:00 hours.

PART 2:
GREENWICH MEAN TIME

Military time won't eliminate *all* misunderstandings about time, though, since spies work all around the world, and they have to communicate across lots of different time zones. And that's

not all: Daylight Savings Time can confuse things, too. So, to clear all this up, spies will agree to use the same time, no matter where they are in the world. And that's where Greenwich Mean Time (otherwise known as GMT) comes in. What's that? Check out the world map above, and you'll see Greenwich. That's a town in England, and it's the home of GMT. Depending on where you are in the world, your time will be a certain number of hours behind or ahead of GMT. Follow these steps to figure out what time it is right now (as you read this very page!) in GMT.

1 First, you have to figure out if you're in Daylight Savings Time or Standard Time. Here's a hint: Daylight Savings Time runs from April through October, roughly. Some places don't observe it, though, so ask an adult if you're not sure. If you're in Standard Time, you're already a step ahead (so go to step 2 already!). If you're in Daylight Savings Time, you need to convert your time to Standard Time by subtracting one hour from the time. For example, if your time is

14:00 in Daylight Savings Time, then it's 13:00 in Standard Time.

2 Next, convert your local Standard Time to Greenwich Mean Time by using the map on page 38. The map shows the time zones of the world in different colors. So, find your time zone and then look at the bottom of the map for the nearest matching color band. There you'll find the number of hours your time is different from GMT. If you're to the left of Greenwich (that is, to the west), then you're behind GMT, and you'll have to add the number of hours to your time. If you're to the right of Greenwich (that is, to the east), then you're ahead of GMT, and you'll have to subtract the number of hours from your time. So, for example, if you're on the East Coast of the United States, you'll have to add five hours to your Standard Time to get GMT. **Note:** Some areas have special times, like India, which is five and a *half* hours ahead of GMT. Check the map to see if your time zone has a special number in it. If so, that's the number you should add or subtract from your time to find GMT.

MORE FROM HEADQUARTERS

1 Imagine you're in Italy, and you have to set up a phone call with your handler. You want to call him at 8:00 p.m. your local time (and it's the middle of winter, so it's Standard Time). What time would you tell him to expect your call in GMT? Write a secret message to your handler giving him the time (in military form) that you'll be calling. (Check your answer on page 48.)

2 Go to the Spy University web site at **www.scholastic.com/spy** and check the clocks. You can find out what time it is in major cities around the world.

WHAT'S THE SECRET?

If you study a globe closely, you'll notice a grid of lines on its surface. Those are called longitude and latitude lines, and they're used to identify locations around the earth (in "degrees" of latitude and longitude). The longitude lines (which run from the north pole to the south pole) also help set up time zones. The longitude line that runs through the town of Greenwich, England, is used as a standard, because it's a very special longitude line, 0° longitude, also known as the Prime Meridian. It got this honor because of a famous astronomical observatory that's there (which nowadays is the home of a clock that keeps exact Greenwich Mean Time).

Since the earth rotates in a counterclockwise direction, locations to the west of Greenwich are at an earlier time than Greenwich, while locations east of Greenwich are at a later time. As a general rule, you change about one hour of time for every 15° of longitude you move.

(continued from page 34 or 43)

As you ride your bike up to the entrance of Cold Creek Park, you can see that the sun is almost setting. It's a little late to be going to the park, so you hope you're not making a big mistake here. When you reach the entrance, you stop and scan the area for Jordan. Sure enough, you see him in the distance, sitting at one of the picnic tables, unloading some items from his backpack. Good for you! Now you have to decide how best to watch him.

- If you decide to climb one of the trees behind the picnic tables to get a better view, turn to **page 41**.
- If you decide to conduct your surveillance from the park's entrance, turn to **page 47**.

OPERATION quick change

Spies are experts at disguises. They know lots of clever ways to change how they look in order to stay undercover. A quick disguise can help a spy in a lot of tricky situations, like when she thinks a spy catcher (or in other words, a **counterspy**) is following her and she needs to slip out of sight, or when she's following someone, and she thinks he might be on to her. Quick getaway maneuvers like these are part of the **tradecraft** spies call "E & E," or **escape and evasion**. Try this activity yourself, and see what a simple quick change can do!

STUFF YOU'LL NEED

- **Jacket that's a different color than your shirt**
- **Backpack**
- **Watch**

YOUR NETWORK

A friend who wants to play a little hide-and-seek (a spy catcher)

WHAT YOU DO

1 Prepare a "quick change" bag by putting your jacket in your backpack. Don't tell your spy catcher about this!

2 In a school yard, crowded hallway, or busy park (or any other safe place where there are lots of people), choose a spot for your spy catcher to stand. Give him the watch (or, better yet, make sure he has his own).

3 Tell your spy catcher to turn around and wait thirty seconds (using the watch). When he's finished waiting, he should turn around and try to spot you in the crowd. When he does, he should shout, "I see you!" and check his watch to see how long it took to spot you.

4 While your spy catcher is counting to thirty, go get lost in the crowd.

5 Listen for your spy catcher to shout, "I see you!"

6 Go to the spy catcher and find out how long it took him to spot you.

7 Repeat steps 3 through 6. This will get your spy catcher used to looking for you in your current clothing.

Can you spot the spy?

8 Now you're ready for the quick change! Repeat steps 3 through 6 again, but this time, when your spy catcher turns away, quickly put on your jacket.

9 Your spy catcher, unaware of your quick change, now has to spot you in the crowd again. See how long it takes him this time!

MORE FROM HEADQUARTERS

1 Add a baseball cap to your quick change bag, and put the cap on with the jacket. See how that affects a spy catcher's ability to find you! You can also try this in reverse by starting with a baseball cap and removing it during the quick change.

2 Switch roles with your friend and see how hard it is for you to catch *him* after he has done a quick change.

3 Try other ways of quickly changing your appearance. Try changing the way you walk. Try walking hunched over, then try walking with a limp or with a bounce in your step. How does changing your walk keep others from knowing it's you?

WHAT'S THE SECRET?

A quick change is a surprisingly simple way to throw someone off your tail, and it's all about color. This happens because when someone is trying to pick you out of a crowd (or watch you from a distance), he's focusing on a few key things like the color of your clothes or whether you're wearing a hat or not. If your friend remembers you with a yellow shirt and blue baseball cap, he will have a tough time spotting you if you switch to a red jacket and take off the cap.

Spies use tricks like wearing reversible jackets, keeping glasses in their pockets, and carrying hats to change their appearance in the wink of an eye. That way, if they're being followed, they can quickly turn a corner, make a slight change of appearance, and slip away undetected.

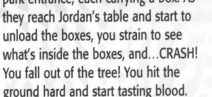

SPYquest

(continued from page 39)

Leaving your bike on the bike rack near the park's entrance, you sneak over to a tree and climb it. You get pretty high up, so you can watch as Jordan puts a yellow paper tablecloth on the table, then plates, napkins, and forks. You're wondering what this is all about when, in the distance, you see a woman and an older boy approaching from the park entrance, each carrying a box. As they reach Jordan's table and start to unload the boxes, you strain to see what's inside the boxes, and...CRASH! You fall out of the tree! You hit the ground hard and start tasting blood. You've bitten your lip pretty badly. You're lucky you didn't knock any teeth out!

Fortunately, Jordan and the others don't see you, but you know you'd better get home to clean up your bloody lip.

■ Ouch! That was definitely a dead end. Turn back to **page 11** and try again!

OPERATION ALPHABET SLIDE

Congrats—you've almost completed your introduction to espionage! This final mission will take you into the world of secret **codes** and **ciphers**. A cipher is a form of code in which a new set of letters (or numbers) is substituted for the real letters of your message. The message ends up looking like gibberish instead of actual words! Historians believe that Julius Caesar, the leader of the Roman Empire in 50 B.C.E., invented the following cipher. So, try Caesar's cipher and see how a simple alphabet slide can turn a SECRET into a PBZOBQ!

STUFF YOU'LL NEED

- **Sheet of lined paper**
- **Pencil**

YOUR NETWORK

A friend to receive your practice messages

WHAT YOU DO

1 Turn the sheet of lined paper sideways, so that the lines form columns.

2 Write out the alphabet from A to Z, putting one letter in each column.

3 Now you're going to write the

alphabet a second time, underneath the first alphabet, but start by putting the letter A under the upper alphabet's letter D, so that the whole alphabet shifts to the right by three letters. Continue writing the lower alphabet until you get to the letter W, which will be

ABCDEFGHIJKLMNOPQRSTUVWXYZ
ABCDEFGHIJKLMNOPQRSTUVW

SPYquest

(continued from page 21)

You ride your bike to 224 Boswell Street, arriving right around 4:00 p.m. To your surprise, it's a women's hair salon. What would Jordan be doing here? Just then, you look in the window and see none other than Jordan's teacher sitting in one of the hairdresser's chairs, with her hair all wet and piled on top of her head in clips. Yikes! Just what you didn't need to see! But before you can duck away, she turns to see you standing in the window. She waves hello, looking a bit surprised to see you

there. You quickly hide the sheet of paper you took from her pad and try not to look too guilty.

■ Oops. This was definitely a dead end. Turn back to **page 11** and start again.

A B C D E F G H I J K L M N O P Q R S T U V W X Y Z
X Y Z A B C D E F G H I J K L M N O P Q R S T U V W

underneath the Z from the upper alphabet. Then go back to the start of the upper alphabet and finish writing the X, Y, and Z of the lower alphabet. That's the Caesar cipher!

4 To encode a message (that is, to turn a message into code), look for the letter you want to encode in the top alphabet. The letter below is the one you'll write in code. For example, the word SPY would be PMV in this code. Try it yourself. How would you write HELLO in this code?

5 To decode a message (translate a coded message into plain language), you just reverse the process in step 4. Let's try another example. How would you decode the message, **PBZOBQ JBBQFKD QLKFDEQ**?

6 Check your answers for steps 4 and 5 in the **What's the Secret?** section in the next column.

7 In order to use this code to send a message, you'll have to teach the recipient how to decode it. Once you've done that, you're all set to communicate Caesar style. Give it a try!

MORE FROM HEADQUARTERS

1 Try shifting the letters of the lower alphabet more or less to the right to change the code. You just have to make sure to tell the person who's receiving the code how many letters to shift the alphabet. (And do it secretly! You might even try using invisible ink, like you learned in **Operation Invisible Ink** on page 28. Just write the number of letters invisibly in the corner of the page.)

2 Your friend sends you the following secret messages. Can you decode them? (You can find the answers in the Answer Spot on page 48.

Don't peek until you've actually done your own decoding!)

a. **IBXSB IBQBO RKABO ALLO**
b. **JBBQ EXKAIBO QLJLOOLT**

3 Visit the Spy University web site at **www.scholastic.com/spy** and try out the cipher machine!

WHAT'S THE SECRET?

HELLO should be written EBIIL as a cipher. The cipher message, **PBZOBQ JBBQFKD QLKFDEQ**, would be "Secret meeting tonight."

Historians believe that Julius Caesar used this simple cipher when writing important messages. This time we've shifted the alphabet three letters to the right, but no matter how many letters you shift the alphabet, it's still called the Caesar cipher.

(continued from page 21 or 36)

Since it's the end of the day, there's a lot of junk in the trash can, but you start digging. At the very bottom, below lots of gross gum and pencil shavings and drippy lunch bags, you find the crumbled-up wad of paper. You open it up, and you find the following row of letters:

JBBQ XQ ZLIA ZOBBH MXOH XQ PRKPBQ

Below the row of letters there are a lot of erasures and cross-outs, so it seems like Jordan was trying to figure out a code. It looks like he was having a rough time, too. You immediately recognize the code, though, since you've just been learning about this kind of thing in Spy University. Perfect!

■ If you decide to go to Cold Creek Park at sunset, turn to **page 39**.

■ If you decide to go to Cold Creek Park on Sunday, turn to **page 29**.

Spying THROUGH THE AGES

Now's your chance to find out when and where spying got started, so here we go, back in time and around the world. Buckle up!

Although we don't really know when the very first spy uncovered the very first bit of intelligence, we *do* know that spying has been around since ancient times. More than 3,400 years ago, the Hebrew leaders Moses and Joshua each used spies to gather the information they needed to plan an invasion of Canaan (modern-day Israel). Of the two leaders, Joshua made the best use of his spies, as Moses's spies reported their findings in public, which caused a great deal of alarm and confusion. Joshua had his spies report to him in *private*, and he was able to use their information to conquer Jericho (a city in Canaan). For this, Joshua is considered the first effective **spymaster** in history.

About 2,500 years ago, the Chinese general Sun Tzu wrote a book about military tactics called *The Art of War*. In part of the book, he discussed the importance of spies. He wrote that an army should advance only when it knew the enemy's strengths. This was impossible

Sun Tzu

without spies. Sun Tzu described how a spy could use deception to trick others into giving up the information he needed. The general also described how to use money to buy information. Sun Tzu even sent spies into enemy territory with false information so that when the spies were captured and forced to confess everything, they would mislead the enemy! Many of Sun Tzu's ideas are still being used today.

Sir Francis Walsingham

Many elements of modern **espionage** had their origins with Sir Francis Walsingham, Secretary of State for Queen Elizabeth I of England in the mid-1500s. Walsingham ran a **spy network** that was very successful in gaining access to the secrets of England's enemies. England was a Protestant country with a weak army, and it was constantly threatened by Catholic countries such as France and Spain (which had much stronger armies). There were also threats from within by those who wanted to overthrow Elizabeth's rule. Walsingham used both espionage and **counterintelligence** to defeat a number of plots to overthrow the queen.

George Washington had an organization of spies that helped him in the American Revolutionary War (1775–1783). Many of the spies who worked during the American Revolution had little formal training. One Revolutionary War spy, Nathan Hale, gathered information on the British army. He was eventually captured by the British (who executed him), but just before he died he said a very famous line: "I only regret that I have but one life to lose for my country."

Then there's the story of Benedict Arnold, the traitor who spied for the British during the Revolutionary War. Arnold began the war as an American hero, leading his Connecticut militia to victory in several battles against the British. But Arnold also had a huge ego and felt slighted when he was passed over for promotion to the rank of Major General of the Revolutionary Army. Angered, he then became a spy for the British, even though he was commander of an American military post at West Point, New York.

HIDDEN NOTE

Arnold would give military secrets to his **handler**, the British spy John Andre, who would hide the secrets in his boot. When Andre was captured by American soldiers (and the secret papers from Arnold were found in his boot), Arnold was forced to flee to the British. He ended up fighting for the British army for the rest of the war.

During the American Civil War (1861–1865), both the Union and Confederate armies used spies to gather information. Photography was introduced into spying during this time. It was so new that few military commanders saw it as a threat. As a result, photographers were allowed to openly take pictures of military defenses, and both sides gathered information this way. In one of the more unusual spying techniques of this time, hydrogen-filled balloons were raised 300 feet (91 m) above the ground, giving Union observers a 15-mile (24-km) view for gathering information about the enemy.

CAMERA
click!

During World War I, the use of cameras in espionage rose to new heights—that is, into airplanes. Photography from planes became so important and widespread that by 1917 armies stopped moving in daylight. Otherwise, their movements would be easily photographed by spy planes overhead. In fact, the first fighter planes came into play during this time in order to keep spy planes from being shot down.

Espionage also played a key role in World War II. The breaking of German and Japanese secret **codes** had a huge influence on the outcome of the war. Interested? The upcoming Spy University book, the *Spy's Guide to Secret Codes and Ciphers*, will tell you all about it.

World War II also saw the establishment of the first centralized intelligence agency in the United States. At the start of the war in Europe in 1939, Germany, Japan, the Soviet Union, and Britain had well-established intelligence services. The United States did not. Recognizing it was behind, the United States founded the Coordinator of Information in 1941, which became the Office of Strategic Services (OSS) in 1942. The role of the OSS was intelligence gathering and secret warfare.

Since then, intelligence networks have become major operations for most governments around the world. Here are just a few of them:

CIA crest

■ In the United States, the CIA (Central Intelligence Agency), the DIA (Defense Intelligence Agency), and the NSA (National Security Agency) all handle espionage and terrorism outside of the United States. The FBI (the Federal Bureau of Investigation) investigates terrorism and foreign espionage *within* the United States.

■ In Israel, the intelligence service is Mossad (which means "institute" in Hebrew—short for the Central Institute for Intelligence and Special Tasks).

SVR crest

■ In Russia, it's the SVR (which is the Russian abbreviation for Russian Foreign Intelligence Service).

■ Canada's intelligence needs are handled by CSIS (Canadian Security Intelligence Service).

■ The intelligence service in Great Britain is MI6 (which stands for Military Intelligence 6, but the agency is called by its official name, the Secret Intelligence Service). MI5 handles counterintelligence, like the FBI in the United States.

MI5 crest

So, we're done with our journey through the history of spying. Do you have any questions? Of course you do! Spies like you have inquiring minds! But never fear, we'll be back each month with a new book that'll have more stories from the world of espionage. And if you can't wait, you can always conduct a little investigation yourself! Who knows what you might find out?

FBI headquarters, Washington, D.C.